The Great Little
GREEN BOOK
of
AFFORMATIONS®

**INCREDIBLY SIMPLE QUESTIONS -
AMAZINGLY POWERFUL RESULTS
FOR GROWING YOUR
CHIROPRACTIC PRACTICE!**

NOAH ST. JOHN & DENISE BERARD
Founder and CEO,
The Success Clinic of America

Also by Noah St. John & Denise Bérard
Permission to Succeed®
Permission to Succeed® *Audio Learning System*
The Great Little Book of Afformations®
(New Expanded Edition)
The Great Little Pink Book of Afformations®
(for Independent Business Professionals)
The Great Little Wellness Book of Afformations®

Published by MetaPublishing
1350 Lakeview Avenue, Dracut MA 01826
Includes Table of Contents
ISBN 0-9715629-4-6

DENISE'S DEDICATION

To my Dad, Alphee J. Cassista, D.C.
who taught me how to live
Thank you for that most precious gift.

To my brother Gerard Cassista, D.C.
who taught me how to laugh
The fun never ends!

To my son, Christopher J. Berard, D.C.
whose courage and integrity make me so proud
(and who has the world's best hugs)

And to my grandson, Connor Hughes
who wants to be a Chiropractor and Spiderman
when he grows up.

I love you all...

ACKNOWLEDGEMENTS

Special thanks to:

God, for making all things possible.

Dr. Al Cassista, for being the best Dad, my best friend, and the perfect example of what love and healing really are in this world.

Mrs. Gabrielle Cassista, for being the best Mom in the whole world. Really. I checked.

Dr. Chris Berard, Dr. Gerard Cassista, Dr. Robert Mugavero and Dr. Shannon Schaffner for their editorial support, love and encouragement. We're so grateul for your wonderful insights and contributions.

Mike, Nicole, Connor and Brianna Hughes, for being such great sports in posing for our cover photograph. I'm sure your Pépère is proud to have "his Nickie" on the cover of this little book.

Steve and Carol Hrehovcik for being great parents and always believing in us and everything we do.

Charna Buchbinder-Zeller, our most faithful friend and Loving Mirror.

Jack Canfield, for his vital role in helping to get the *Permission to Succeed*® and *Afformations*® teachings into the hands of people around the world.

Dr. John Gray, for his loving support and belief in our mission.

Dr. Fabrizio Mancini, for his radiant warmth and strength of vision.

Louise Bérard, photographer *extraordinaire* and constant giver of love.

Dave Wagoner, for his wonderfully creative cover design of our Afformations Book series.

Scott Zimmerman, for his zany sense of humor and for The Cyrano System, which keeps us in touch with clients around the world every day.

The authors of the original Green Books, whose epigrams appear at the end of chapters throughout this book.

St. Paul, St. Anthony, St. Jude, St. Theresa and Solomon, who have never let us down.

Our thousands of dedicated students worldwide. We learn so much from working with each of you.

Contents

PREFACE TO
CHIROPRACTIC EDITION

The Afformations book you are holding is part of an ongoing series of *Great Little Afformations Books*. For information on the other books in the series, as well as other tools to help you live the life of your dreams, visit **SuccessClinic.com.**

This special chiropractic edition contains stories, examples and questions not found in the original *Great Little Book of Afformations*, first published in 2001.

Since the original publication, countless people from around the world have told us their stories of how afformations have changed their lives.

The story of the discovery of afformations, along with the essential teaching, remains fundamentally the same throughout the series. Each book, however, is unique. Whether you're a student just starting out or have been in practice for years, if you want to learn an easy way to put Infinite Intelligence to work for you, this book is just what the doctor ordered!

HOW THIS BOOK WAS WRITTEN – AND WHY

Did you ever notice how the best ideas come to you in the shower?

It happens all the time – you're minding your own business, holding the shampoo bottle – when suddenly, it hits you.

The idea that's going to change everything.

The solution to the problem you're facing.

The answer to the question you've been asking.

And it was right in front of you all along...

This book tells the story of what can happen to you when something like that happens to you!

April, 1997. A crisp spring morning like any other in New England. I was living in a dorm room at the college where I was a religious studies major.

The dorm room itself was sizable enough, in that, simply by standing in the middle of the room, I could touch the walls on both sides.

At that point, I realized that something was wrong with my life.

At that point in my life – as a divorced 30-year-old religious studies major living in a tiny dorm room of a baroque New England college – I realized that something was wrong, amazingly wrong, with my life.

I had been studying self-help books since I was a little boy, having pulled Dale Carnegie's *How to Win Friends and Influence People* off the shelf at age seven. (A well-meaning editor told me to leave that story out of one of my previous books, because, she told me, no one would believe it.) Yet something was missing. Something was gnawing at me, telling me that the

answer I'd been seeking was somewhere out there –
that I just had to keep looking for it.

Then, The Shower happened.

The night before, I'd been looking around my
diminuitive dorm room and realized that I had posted
lots of sayings or "affirmations" around the room to
make myself feel better; things like, *"I am happy, healthy
and wealthy"* and *"I am good enough."*

Funny, but for some reason, I never quite believed
what I had spent so much time saying to myself.

So, on the morning of The Shower, I was asking
myself some simple but profound questions.
Questions like:

*"If I keep saying these 'affirmations' and have been saying
them over and over for so long, why don't I believe them?"*

*"If I've been saying positive statements to myself for years,
how come I still don't feel good about myself?"*

And: *"There must be a better way to get myself to believe
something good about me. But what is it?"*

And then it hit me. (No, not the soap.)

I realized that the human brain is always asking
and searching for answers to questions. In other

words, you could say that *thought itself is the process of asking and searching for the answers to questions.*

If that's true, I reasoned, then there was a simple question that followed – a simple question that changed everything. The question was this:

"If human thought is really the process of asking and searching for answers to <u>questions</u>, why are we going around making <u>statements</u> we don't believe?"

I couldn't think of a good answer to that question.

That's when everything changed for me– and for the tens of thousands of people around the globe who've since learned how to apply what I discovered in The Shower. You'll learn what happened next – and how you can benefit from my discovery – in the pages that follow.

Enjoy!

To your Success,
Noah St. John, Founder
SuccessClinic.com

~ ~ ~

How this book was written—and why

Dear Friend,

When I was six years old, my parents packed up the car with my four brothers and sisters and everything we owned, and took off to Davenport, Iowa. My Dad, then almost 40, had always dreamed of becoming a chiropractor, and he was about to make that dream come true. We moved into converted army barracks called Palmerton and off to Palmer College he went.

After my Dad graduated, we all moved back to Massachusetts. Unfortunately, chiropractic wasn't as yet legal in that state, forcing him to practice in New Hampshire. All the while, my Dad championed for the cause, writing to Congressmen and Senators, attending fundraisers and speaking out to raise public awareness of chiropractic.

My Dad and I had a very special connection. I worked in his office, stuffed awareness letters for him by the thousands, and went along with him to every event.

You might wonder why a young girl would be so

passionate about the cause. It was so much more to me than legalization of chiropractic – it was about getting this care to the millions of people who needed it. It came from seeing the little boy gasping with asthma until my father adjusted him on the bleachers so he could return to his Little League game...

It came from hearing the unforgettable excitement in the voice of a new mom who previously had no sense of touch, as she called my Dad's office crying and exclaimed that she had just dropped her baby's bottle, felt the pain on her foot and the warmth of the milk...

My passion was about the people, the faces and the lives I saw my father change.

It came from knowing the little girl – the one whose nervous condition was so severe that her parents had been told she'd never be able to function with other children – calm down, find peace and join society as a normal child.

My passion was about the people, the faces and the lives I saw my father change. Chiropractic was not my Dad's profession – it was his way of life.

My younger brother, Dr. Gerard Cassista, went on to follow in my Dad's footsteps. He has the same loving, generous spirit I saw in my father. Dr. Gerry now has one of the most successful chiropractic practices in New England and has just taken on an associate, my wonderful son, Dr. Christopher Berard.

Each time I see Dr. Chris give his patients a big hug after an adjustment, I get all filled up just knowing how proud his grandfather would be of him.

And we may even have a fourth generation chiropractor in the wings: Connor, my four-year-old grandson (who appears on the cover) always wants to adjust us, and says he wants to be just like Uncle Chris and Great Uncle Gerry!

I think you can see just how much this book means to me, and how proud and honored I feel to be giving you this gift of my soul. Chiropractic runs through every inch of my being and I feel most blessed to share this work with you.

When we first began working on this book, we weren't sure what to call it. We had at first considered

The Great Little Chiropractic Book of Afformations. When we asked the advice of several chiropractor friends, it appeared unanimous. Everyone said it just had to be *The Great Little Green Book of Afformations* in honor of the incredible work done by the visionaries who created the foundational Green Book series.

This *Little Green Book* was written for you if you are one of the tens of thousands of practitioners who:

• Want more control, more freedom and more abundance in every area of your life

• Are seeking to enhance the balance between your faith, your family and your career

• Want to create a better life for those around you

• Are seeking to reach a higher level of compassion, integrity and honor in your life

• Want to find a better way to express all that you are and all that you hope to become

• Want to experience oneness with Universal Intelligence.

This little book holds the answers to questions you may have had for years – and provides answers to questions you didn't even know you had!

It's our honor to share these secrets with you, just as it's been our honor and privilege to show countless people and organizations in America and worldwide, how to get better results with less effort.

Please give yourself and your loved ones the gift of allowing this little book to change your life (and theirs), and enjoy a life of true abundance!

Best wishes on your journey,
Denise Berard, CEO
SuccessClinic.com

Introduction

TOP 10 WAYS TO GET THE MOST FROM THIS BOOK

A book should be luminous, not voluminous.
– Oliver Wendell Holmes

1. Read it through all at once.

This book is short on purpose. We know you're busy. We've designed it to fit easily in your purse or briefcase. You won't find any complex psychological theories here (well, just one – but we explain it pretty quickly and it's easy to understand).

2. Set the book down and let your mind wander.

Once you've read it through the first time, put it away for a while. Take a walk. Let ideas come to you.

3. Highlight the passages that have special meaning to you.

Did a certain phrase or question bring up strong emotions in you? Underline or highlight those passages so you can refer to them later. Also, write the date next to the text you've highlighted, so that each time you revisit this book, you'll see just how far you've come.

4. Use the questions in this book to guide you, but don't feel limited by them.

We learn better when we teach.

In Chapter 3, you'll learn how to create empowering questions of your own. Remember, you are creating your life right now by the questions you're asking - why not make them work <u>for you</u>!

5. Teach this technique <u>twice</u>.

We all learn better when we teach. Research suggests that when you teach this method at least twice in the next 48 hours – once to your loved ones and once to your business colleagues – not only will you personally be better able to apply this teaching, you'll also be socially committed to the teaching, which will make it that much harder for you to go back to the old, disempowering way of thinking.

6. Allow the method to be as easy as it is.

You may be surprised because what you're going to be doing isn't hard. You may even feel somewhat embarrassed, because sometimes it won't even feel like you're doing anything.

You may believe you have to work hard to get the results you want. Sure, you often need to work hard and sacrifice to get what you want. But consider that many of the most important things in the world – love, peace, serenity – often appear, not because we work hard at them, but because we <u>allow</u> them.

7. Yet, don't be fooled by how easy this method appears.

Tens of thousands of people with whom we've shared this method have told us that this process has changed their lives in ways both immediate and long-lasting. But just because it's easy doesn't mean you don't have to do <u>anything</u>. You will have to change many of the things you've been thinking and saying to yourself, perhaps for most of your life. This method will work just as well for you as it has for the thousands of people we've heard from, if you trust yourself and trust the method.

8. Do the exercises in the book.

You can't do 20 push-ups merely by reading a book about how to do it. You have to roll up your sleeves and do it. You'll find that the benefits of doing the simple exercises we suggest will far outweigh the pain of having done them. Really.

9. Write and share your experiences with us.

We love to read your success stories! Write and share them with us. We're also here to help any time you have questions.

10. Finally, remember your job on Earth is to serve others and be blessed in the process.

As you bless others, the blessings will return to you, too. There's plenty to go around, and through this method, you'll learn how to let abundance manifest in your own life. Share the gift of YOU with others, and watch your own life and the lives of those around you change for the better… for good!

1

WHY TRADITIONAL "AFFIRMATIONS" DON'T ALWAYS WORK AS ADVERTISED

*Every sentence I utter must be understood
not as an affirmation, but as a question.*
– Niels Bohr, Nobel Prize winning physicist

Have you ever wanted to change your life? If you want more control over your practice, more money to enjoy the fruits of your labor, or more freedom to do the things you really want to do, the answer is almost certainly "yes."

Well, if you wanted to change your life, what have you tried to do differently? If you're like many people, you may have tried:

- Beginning a new diet/exercise program
- Reading self-help books
- Listening to self-improvement CDs or tapes
- Working on your communication skills
- Writing your goals
- Trying to get support from your spouse
- Writing or saying "affirmations"

Hey, what's that last one! A great many of us have tried using "affirmations" to change our lives – but the questions is: why?

Because that's what a lot of very successful people have told you to do. For decades, many very successful people have built fortunes persuading you and me and millions of others about the importance of using "affirmations" to change your life.

The second question we should be asking when it comes to "affirmations" is: *do they really work?*

The answer is: sometimes.

Wouldn't it be helpful to know what actually makes "affirmations" work – and what makes them sometimes NOT work?

HOW THE HUMAN MIND WORKS

Consider this: the human mind has created every work of art, poetry, science, religion, philosophy, mathematics, history, and romance that has ever existed. Here are just a few of the things you can do with your wonderful mind:

Arrange, blueprint, chart, construct, create, design, devise, discover, dream up, engineer, evoke, fabricate, fashion, form, frame, generate, hatch, imagine, improvise, invent, lead, manipulate, make up, mastermind, originate, produce, provoke, plan, plot, prepare, rig, scheme, shape, spark, think, throw together, whip up, work out.

Isn't that amazing? And you can do all that before breakfast!

We often think of ourselves as being static, fixed, unchanging beings: "I am what I am and that's that." But think a new thought for a moment. Have you ALWAYS been that way? Were you the way you are now when you first learned to walk…first learned to ride a bicycle…went to your first day of school…opened your first bank account…went on your first date…had your first child?

All of these stages in life meant one thing: CHANGE. You had to accept a new reality when you went from crawling to walking…from being dependent on your parents to being independent…from working for someone else to starting your own business!

So your life really is the process of changing from one set of circumstances to another (hopefully better) set of circumstances.

Now, here's where it gets interesting…

WHAT THE TRADITIONAL SUCCESS TEACHERS TOLD YOU

What is an "affirmation"? Simply put, an *affirmation* is a statement of something you'd like to be true in your life.

William James, often called the father of modern psychology, has been widely quoted as saying, "The greatest discovery of my generation is that anyone can alter their lives by altering their attitudes of mind." What's rarely pointed out, however, is that since William James died in 1910, that means several generations have had the chance to "alter" their lives by changing their thoughts.

Your thoughts are seeds that you plant every minute of every day, whether you know it or not.

Your thoughts are very literal *seeds* that you plant every minute of every hour of every day, whether you're aware of it or not. These thought-seeds are planted (whether or not you're aware of them) in the fertile soil of Infinite Intelligence, which simply takes your thought-seeds and hands them back to you as Your Life.

You would think, then, with the millions of self-help books published that support this notion, that by now we'd all know how to change our lives simply by changing our attitudes of mind.

All you have to do is look around you to see that, unfortunately, that's not exactly the case. Yet.

The question is...
Why not?

WHAT TRADITIONAL SUCCESS TEACHERS <u>FORGOT</u> TO TELL YOU

Let's say you're having trouble with money and you'd like to change that. (Actually, the only "trouble" with money is that you have some, and everyone else has all the rest.) And let's say that you've been raised on the traditional method just described, which says that in order to change your life, you must first change your thoughts.

Makes sense so far. You know and realize the truth of the statement, "As you sow, so shall you reap," the fact that <u>thoughts are the seeds you plant</u>.

And let's say that you went back to your childhood and realized that you grew up experiencing lack, and identified that the thought that's holding you back is, *"I don't have enough."*

Now that you've identified the main thought that's been holding you back, you realize that your next step is to *change that thought*. In other words, you want to stop planting negative thought-seeds (what you don't want) and start planting positive thought-seeds (what you want).

So now you begin to do what the traditional success teachers have been telling you: start using "affirmations" or positive statements. Why? Because you're trying to change your thoughts, and naturally the way to do that is to say, write or think different statements – changing the negative to positive.

So, to combat the negative thought-seed of *"I don't have enough,"* you begin saying, writing and thinking the positive thought-seed of *"I have enough"* or even, *"I am rich."*

And, because you're such a good student, you do this over and over and over...which would change your attitude, which would change your results, which would mean your money problems are over!

Right?

~ ~ ~

All right, let's try it.

Say to yourself right now, *"I am rich."*
Say it again.
"I am rich."
What just happened in your mind?
Did you hear something else in there?
A voice... a voice that said something like...
"Yeah, right."

Let me ask you a question - friend to friend:
Do you honestly believe your own "affirmations"
– or do you doubt them?

The plain and simple truth is that many of us
doubt our own "affirmations." Why? *Because you're*
trying to convince yourself of something you don't believe is true.

Now, traditional success teachers realized that you
may not believe that you are, in fact, rich and that you
do, in fact, have enough. So they told you, with very
good intentions, that all you had to do was repeat
your "affirmations" a million kajillion times until,
eventually, you believed them.

Have you ever realized you were holding onto a
negative thought (for example, *"I'm poor, I'm lonely, I*

don't have enough")…decided you wanted something better…wrote and said positive "affirmations" (for example, *"I am rich, I'm happy, I have enough"*)…

And then had…

Absolutely nothing happen?

Me too. And about a gazillion other people.

Why? If it were as easy as they said, why did nothing happen? Were we simply incapable of thinking a positive thought? Were we not smart enough, not motivated enough, not educated enough…or did we just not try hard enough?

Dear friend, the answer is none of these.

The answer is: you were using conscious statements when your subconscious mind responds to <u>questions</u>.

You were trying to overcome negative beliefs using statements, when it's so much easier to overcome them using <u>questions</u>.

You were <u>telling</u> when you should have been <u>asking</u>.

What on Earth do we mean?

2

AFFORMATIONS® - A NEW WAY
TO ASK POSITIVE QUESTIONS
FOR GREATER RESULTS

I don't pretend to have all the answers.
But the questions are sure worth thinking about.
– Arthur C. Clarke, author of
2001: A Space Odyssey

Did you see what just happened? We ended the last chapter with something that made you curious: a question. The dictionary defines "question" as: "an expression of inquiry that calls for a reply." So when you ask yourself a question, what happens?

For example, right now, you may be asking yourself, "I don't know – what happens?"

Your mind automatically began Searching for an answer to your question.

WHAT EVERY PROBLEM YOU'LL EVER FACE REALLY IS

Do you know what every problem you'll ever face is? We typically fear, try to avoid, ignore, or get away from problems. But really, a problem is simply *a question that hasn't been answered yet.*

Any problem, from the trivial to the tremendous, is really a question searching for an answer. Here are a few serious global problems and their associated questions:

The homeless: "Where can we house all the people who have no means to pay for shelter?"

Poverty: "How can we equally distribute the wealth of the world so that people don't have to go without the basic necessities of life?"

Unemployment: "How can we get everyone working in jobs that produce wealth for themselves and help society function better as well?"

(Notice we didn't say these were easy questions. That's why we haven't found all the answers yet!)

What about the problems we face on the personal or professional level?

Wanting to be more successful: "How can I be more successful in my life and business?"

Lack of organization: "Why can't I find what I'm looking for?"

Wanting companionship: "Why can't I meet the person of my dreams?"

If you'd like to change any of these, you could use the traditional "affirmation" method by saying things like: *"I am a success." "I am organized." "I don't procrastinate."*

You may believe these statements, and you may not. Many people have responded to "affirmations" like these in a simple manner: by not believing them (the *"Yeah, right"* response).

Now, if "affirmations" work for you, that's great! If, however, you're not totally satisfied with the results, why not try something so simple, yet so powerful, that the traditional teachers skipped right over it on the way to breakfast:

Rather than making a statement you may not believe, why not ask yourself a question that can transform your life!

HOW YOU CREATE YOUR LIFE

✳

You create your reality by the <u>statements</u> you say to yourself and others, and by the <u>questions</u> you ask yourself and others.

The staggering realization I made in The Shower on that fateful morning in 1997 was that you are creating the reality of your life at this very moment in two ways: by the statements you say to yourself and others, and by *the questions you ask yourself and others*.

Traditional success teachers have focused a great deal of energy telling you to change your statements. But until The Shower happened to me, no one had fully realized, or shown how to harness, the awesome power of what happens when you change the *questions*.

Your mind has what you might call an *Automatic Search Function*, which means that when you ask yourself a question, your mind automatically begins to Search for an answer. (Psychologists have referred to this function of the human brain as the "embedded presupposition factor.")

The greatest teachers throughout history have taught the truth of the statement, "As you sow, so shall you reap." This is often called The Law of Sowing and Reaping (Emerson called it "First Law"), which means that what you focus on (the thought-seeds you continually plant) will grow and bear fruit.

As we've seen, traditional teachers told you to change your thinking if you want to change your life. And that's quite correct.

What they said, however, was to change the statements you're making, yet almost completely ignored the questions you're asking.

Yet the Bible tells us, "You have not because you ask not," and "Ask and you shall receive."

If you only change the <u>statements</u> you say without changing the <u>questions</u> you ask, you're missing out on one of the easiest, yet most powerful ways to change your life that's ever been discovered!

HOW A 13-YEAR-OLD GIRL CURED HER COMPULSIVE WORRYING

We got a call one day from Mary, a professional salesperson from Beaver Dam, Wisconsin who had attended one of our *Permission to Succeed*® workshops. The first words out of her mouth were, "Your work has been life-changing to me!" When I asked her what she meant, she told me the following story:

After attending your workshop and learning how to use afformations, I realized that if it could work for me, it could also work for my 13-year-old daughter Stefanie. She's a high achiever who gets all A's in school, but she's also a chronic and compulsive worrier.

Stefanie worried so much that she had severe sleeping problems. She'd lay awake many nights worrying, until finally she'd come into our bedroom and wake us from a sound sleep so we could comfort her.

We tried everything. We read to her. We prayed with her. We were even considering taking her to therapy. Still the worrying - and the sleepless nights - continued. She would cry and ask me, "Why do I worry so much?" It broke my heart because I couldn't help my own daughter.

Finally, when I heard you teach afformations at your *Permission to Succeed* workshop, I realized this could be the answer I'd been praying for! When I came back from your workshop, I taught Stefanie how to use afformations, and we talked for a long time about what questions would make the most difference in her life.

She was as excited as I was! The questions we came up with were:

"Why am I worry free?"

"Why do I enjoy a full night's sleep?
"Why do I put trust in God's hands?"
"Why do all my friends love me?"
"Why do I love me?"

Now she's a different kid!

From the very first day she started using afformations - it was truly miraculous, like turning on a dime - Stefanie's worrying stopped. She also became much happier, more relaxed and seems to be at peace in her own skin. And you know how hard that can be for teenagers nowadays - especially teenage girls!

Your *Permission to Succeed* and *Afformations* books were the first self-help books I've ever read where I actually did the exercises. Thank you for making such a difference in our lives!

Mary then told us that not only did afformations improve her own business and enable her daughter to quit worrying, she also started sharing afformations with everyone she met.

When her husband Scott told her that he wasn't

passionate about his work, Mary began afforming, *"Why is the right calling coming to Scott?"* Within weeks, he landed his dream position. And get this: he's working at Stefanie's high school!

EMPOWERING vs. DISEMPOWERING QUESTIONS

Do you know what most people are doing with their lives? Most people are going through life asking negative questions – and wondering why they're not getting the results they dream of!

Let's examine these **empowering** vs. **disempowering questions.** We'll start with disempowering questions, because while they're the kind you may be used to, they're also the ones you want to get rid of immediately.

These are questions like, *"Why am I so afraid? Why doesn't anyone love me? How come I never get the breaks other people get?"* No one says these questions on purpose, but you may be asking them without knowing it.

Now we'd like you to try *consciously* asking these common disempowering questions, and see how you feel: *"Why don't I have enough money? How come I'm so lonely? Why am I such a loser? Why can't I do anything right?"*

As we explain in *Permission to Succeed®*, each of us has a **Negative Reflection** in our subconscious mind – that negative "voice" that tells us we can't do anything right. The Negative Reflection always asks negative or disempowering questions.

The ultimate result of these negative questions is that you will manifest what you focus on. In other words, when you ask yourself negative questions, you get negative results.

Use the space we've given you on the next page to list the five most disempowering questions your Negative Reflection asks you on a regular basis.

Yes, we mean right now.

You'll be amazed at how negative and destructive these questions can be (e.g., *"How come I can't do anything right? Why can't I ever get ahead?, etc."*).

They may have come from someone in your past, or it could be something you made up on your own.

It's vital that you know exactly what your own disempowering questions are, so you can begin to turn them around.

(Note: You might want to write the date next to your questions, so when you come back to this book later, you'll see just how far you've come.)

Please do this right now.

We'll be right here when you get back.

THE 5 MOST DISEMPOWERING QUESTIONS I HEAR IN MY HEAD:

1.

2.

3.

4.

5.

Whew. Pretty bad, aren't they?

Are you ready to find a better way?

EMPOWERING QUESTIONS - THE RIGHT QUESTIONS

Now that you've identified your personal <u>disempowering</u> questions, you may ask, "What are <u>empowering</u> questions – and how can I start asking them instead of the negative ones?"

Glad you asked!

Empowering questions cause your mind to focus on the positive. The only answers to empowering questions are answers or experiences that produce feelings of self-esteem and a positive self-image.

Empowering questions lead to answers that tell the Truth about Who You Really Are.

Empowering questions assume only the best, while disempowering questions assume only the worst.

Let's change your disempowering questions on page 41 to empowering questions. How do you do this? Simply reverse the negative question to a positive.

For example, if your disempowering question is, *"Why am I such a loser?"*, your empowering question would be, *"Why am I such a success?"*

All right, grab your pen and get ready to experience the difference. Here goes...

5 NEW EMPOWERING QUESTIONS I'M GOING TO START ASKING:

1.

2.

3.

4.

5.

Pretty cool, huh?

Did you notice something shift in your mind?

Guess what? You've just begun an amazing journey...

*The purpose of Afformations®
is to change your <u>disempowering</u> questions
to <u>empowering</u> questions.*

*This will give you conscious control
of the thought-seeds you're planting,
which will, through Infinite
Intelligence, change your life.*

YOUNG DOCTOR IN LOVE

We were leading our *Permission to Love™: How to Stop Sabotaging Your Relationships* seminar in Denver and met a young chiropractor who seemed to have everything going for her. She was attractive, intelligent and, by the way she interacted with other audience members, clearly cared about people.

Yet when we asked her to answer questions about herself and her worth in relationships, she burst into tears and told us she couldn't even answer the questions! After having gone through a devastating divorce and other unsuccessful relationships, her self-worth was low and her thoughts for future love were almost hopeless.

The questions in her head went something like this: *"Why have I failed at love? Why does love hurt so much? Why am I unloveable? Why haven't I found the man of my dreams? Why am I not worthy of the love I desire?"*

Guess what her life looked like? Her life had become the literal answer to her disempowering questions! Her subconscious questions had formed a life where she had no confidence in her ability to love and be loved. She began to think that maybe there was no such thing as true, lasting love. It was the definition of a "self-fulfilling prophecy."

The question she began asking was, "Why do I have the most incredibly loving relationship with the man of my dreams?"

Less than three months after the seminar, our phone rang. It was the young doctor. She told us that after the seminar, she realized she was asking herself the wrong questions and had decided to stop. She stopped asking herself negative questions, and began asking herself a single empowering question that changed the way she looked at everything in her life.

The question she asked herself was, *"Why do I have the most incredibly loving relationship with the man of my dreams?"*

As she began asking herself that new question, the Automatic Search Function of her mind began to form new patterns. She started to see things differently, and realized she had been stopping herself from being loved because of the negative questions she'd been asking herself.

She came to realize that a dear friend of hers whom she had known for quite some time, but was several years her junior, was in fact the man of her dreams. She hadn't allowed the possibility to enter her mind because of so many years of disempowering questions.

She decided to take a leap of faith. Her new afformation allowed her to open her mind and heart to the possibility of true love. Today they are happily married and living the life of their dreams. She is also building the chiropractice practice of her dreams. All because she dared to ask herself a new question!

WHY ARE THEY CALLED AFFORMATIONS?

Let's return to what we've learned already: the human mind operates by asking and answering questions. Therefore, when you ask yourself a question repeatedly, *your mind must Search for an answer to your question.*

We call the process of using empowering questions the use of **afformations**, or **The Afformation Method.** So where did the word *afformation* come from?

Noah says: After my discovery in The Shower, I realized the process of asking empowering questions was something that could completely revolutionize the field of self-help and personal development.

I also realized that I had to come up with a word to describe the process of asking empowering questions, so people would be able to fully understand the amazing power of their own minds.

One of my favorite subjects in high school was Latin. (Yes, I was a geek long before they put the word "computer" in front of it.) After The Shower, I discovered that the word "affirmation" comes from the Latin word *firmare*, which means "to make firm." I began asking myself, *"If 'affirmations' are positive statements, what would the perfect word be to describe empowering questions?"*

Then the answer came to me (of course!):

I realized that when we ask questions of ourselves or others – whether positive or negative – we are really FORMING new thought patterns, which can FORM a new life for us.

The word "form" comes from the Latin word *formare,* which means "to form or give shape to."

That's when it hit me: what if you're making something FIRM, but in the wrong FORM?

It was at that moment that I realized the real reason "affirmations" aren't very effective for changing our lives – because we're trying to make something FIRM before we've FORMED what we really want.

I realized that instead of making something FIRM, we needed to FORM questions that would change

When we ask questions, we FORM new thought patterns, which can FORM a new life for us. That's where the word afFORMation came from!

the thought-seeds we were sowing, which would change our lives.

And that's how the word – and the teaching of – AFFORMATIONS® was born.

(By the way, it's perfectly legitimate to invent a new word to describe a new way of looking at the universe. For example, remember the first time you heard the words *Internet, CD-ROM,* or even *software?* Just a few short years ago, these words had no meaning because the technology they describe didn't exist. There was no *context* for the words; no context, no meaning. Now you use those terms every day. We are now learning about a new technology of the mind – hence, AFFORMATIONS: a new word to describe a new technology.)

THE BOTTOM LINE: YOU'RE ALREADY DOING THIS!

In case you're still wondering if this works, or thinking this is the nuttiest thing you've ever heard, let us offer you one final fact:

You are already using
AFFORMATIONS
all the time anyway.

Thoughts like *"Why am I so stupid?"* or *"Why can't I do anything right?"* are simply negative afformations! These questions are really the Negative Reflection <u>forming</u> itself inside your mind, thereby forming your very life.

The power to create your life using afformations lies within you and your miraculous, marvelous mind. You're already using them anyway...why not do it <u>consciously</u> to create the life you <u>want,</u> rather than <u>unconsciously</u> creating a life you <u>don't want</u>?

By the way, if you still doubt the power of afformations, there is a sentence eleven letters long that represents the genesis of every work of art, science, philosophy, and religion in human history.

If you are still not sure whether afformations will work for you, here are the eleven letters that have, in a very real sense, created human history:

"Why am I alive?"

~   ~   ~

You'll find the easiest way to create afformations that can change your life beginning on the next page…

3

HOW TO CREATE AFFORMATIONS THAT CAN CHANGE YOUR LIFE

Take the attitude of a student:
never be too big to ask questions,
never know too much to learn something new.
– Og Mandino
Author of *The Greatest Salesman in the World*

Creating empowering afformations can be one of the most significant steps you'll ever take to gain more control over your practice, raise your self-confidence, improve your personal relationships, or enjoy a deeper relationship with God. Use the following four steps to create powerful afformations that will help you use your mind to create the life you really want:

Step 1: Identify what you want and write it down.

You've probably done this before. In this step, you may go back to goals you've previously written and determine what it is you really want, or start from scratch. You decide.

We've organized this book into 10 major categories of building your practice– from Finding Your Because to Organizing and Delegating to Overcoming Fear, Worry and Frustration. Go through each category and determine what you really want.

(Please note that traditional success literature stops right here. Traditional success teachers have told you to set your goals and then say "affirmations" that attempt to convince your brain that you "will have" or even that you "do have" what you want. While this can also work, The Afformations Method makes reaching your goals so much easier, because it uses your mind's Automatic Search Function to discover positive answers to your new, empowering questions.)

So, for example, you might decide that your goal is to be happy, healthy and wealthy (hard to imagine anyone NOT wanting those things!). So in Step One, you would write: *"I want to be happy, healthy and wealthy."*

Now we go on to the most important step...

Step 2: Form your desire into a <u>question</u> that assumes that what you want <u>is already true</u>.

In Step 2, you start asking a question that <u>assumes</u> that what you want is already so, has already happened, or is already true.

This is the most important step to creating empowering afformations that can change your life!

In the example above, what you want is to be happy, healthy and wealthy, right? Well, in this step you ask yourself WHY this is already so!

Your Life is a reflection of the thought-seeds you plant and give energy to. More precisely, Your Life is a reflection of the <u>unconscious assumptions</u> you make about life and your relationship to it.

There's a mechanism that records and reflects your subconscious thoughts and beliefs. That mechanism is called Your Life.

For example, if you grew up in an environment where there wasn't a lot of money, and your family made you aware that the lack of money was the cause of their unhappiness, you might conclude that there's a lack of money in the world that leads to unhappiness, and that's just the way life is.

If you could find a mechanism that could record your subconscious thought-seeds and play them back to you, they might sound something like this:

"Why am I so unhappy? Why don't I have enough? Why am I so lonely? Why aren't I more successful?", and so forth.

Well, a mechanism <u>does</u> exist that records and reflects your subconscious thought-seeds — that mechanism is called Your Life!

WHAT YOUR LIFE IS

So here you are, asking yourself these often negative questions. What do you think would be the answers to the negative questions in the example above?

The answers would be your life showing up as the negative results of the negative questions you've been asking. For example:

If you've been asking, *"Why am I so unhappy?"*, you'll get the answer as your unhappy life.

If you've been asking, *"Why don't I have enough?"*, the answer will appear as your lack in life.

If you've been asking, *"Why am I so lonely?"*, the person of your dreams will keep not showing up.

REVERSING THE CURSE

When you do this step of The Afformation Method™, you will take what has been subconscious (hidden) and make it conscious (visible), and take what is negative (disempowering) and make it positive (empowering).

Let's reverse all the negative questions from the last page. The reverse might look something like this:

"Why am I so happy? Why do I have enough? Why am I so loved? Why am I so successful?"

These questions may seem unfamiliar to you right now. But what if you allowed yourself to accept those questions as <u>the truth about your life</u>?

Wouldn't you have a life that's different than the average person's — *a life that's different from the one you have now?*

*Your quality of life depends
on just two things:
the quality of your communication
with the world <u>inside</u> yourself,
and the quality of your
communication with the world
<u>outside</u> yourself.*

Step 2 of The Afformations Method is to begin to change the quality of communication with the world <u>inside</u> yourself. You will begin to ask yourself new, better, <u>em</u>powering questions, and stop asking yourself negative, <u>dis</u>empowering questions.

This is the fastest, most effective way we've ever seen that can immediately change the quality of your communication with both your inside and outside worlds.

So Step 2 in The Afformation Method is to ask yourself, *"Why is [what I want] true in my life now?"*

Using our example above, you would ask yourself, *"Why am I so happy, healthy and wealthy?"*

Step 3: Allow your mind to Search for the answers to your question, but don't worry about finding "the answer."

The point of afformations is NOT to answer the question you are presenting! The point is to begin to use your mind in a new way – to begin focusing on things you may never have focused on before.

Noah says: several years ago, I decided I wanted to find my perfect mate. I'd been "looking for love in all the wrong places" and one day, realized I'd been subconsciously asking myself, *"Why can't I find the right woman?"* My life became a reflection of that inner, hidden (negative) question.

The question that came to me was, "Why did she finally come to me... and stay?"

On that day, I decided to change the question I was asking. While meditating, I asked God, "What question should I ask?" The question that came to me was, *"Why did she finally come to me – and stay?"*

I asked myself the new, positive question – in prayer, meditation and journaling. I began to notice that my mind was opening to new possibilities about where to find the love of my life.

Three weeks after I began asking myself *"Why did she finally come to me – and stay?",* I found myself at a networking event two hours from my home. I didn't know a soul in the room. But something told me to go there that night.

In a room filled with over 250 strangers two hours from my home, that's where I met Denise. I had no idea where "she" was going to come from when I began asking the new question. But because I formed a new, empowering question, my mind's Automatic Search Function began to change the assumptions I had made, and the answer manifested as my new life.

So take it from me: afformations really can change your life!

Your mind is like a computer. Once you put your afformation in motion (and <u>keep asking</u> your new, positive questions), your mind will begin to Search for the answer without your conscious volition.

Step 4: Leave your mind alone. Don't wait for an "answer" to your question. Take new <u>actions</u> that come to you as a result of your new assumptions about life!

You are, right now, making assumptions about life and your relationship to it. These assumptions form the basis of how you go through life – with positivity or negativity, confidence or shyness, love or fear, acceptance or resentment.

If you assume that life is <u>for</u> you, the actions you take will be formed from a basis of confidence and the belief that "things will work out for the best." If you assume that life is <u>against</u> you, then your actions will be formed from hesitancy, fear and the belief of "why bother?"

A confident person will have an easier time in life, whether building relationships or building a practice. But where does *confidence* really come from? It comes from the underlying, subconscious assumptions about how life is going to treat you.

The Afformation Method
makes <u>conscious</u> that which has,
until now, been only subconsious.

You are continually forming assumptions about

life and your relationship to it; but these assumptions are nearly always subconscious – so hidden, you don't even realize they're there any more.

As a result, the great percentage of your actions are governed by assumptions you may have formed years – even decades – ago!

If you grew up with the assumption that "life is lack", what would your actions be? How confident would you be about building your practice or meeting new people?

Now what if you were Donald Trump and grew up in the lap of luxury? What would your subconscious assumptions about life be?

Probably something like, *"I can have whatever I want"* or *"There's plenty of money out there, and I have the ability to get it."* In other words, you'd probably believe *"There's more than enough wealth to go around."*

As you can see, someone who believes that "life is lack" is going to do things (take actions) that spring from that assumption. And you can also see that someone like Donald Trump, who grew up with great wealth, is going to literally live in a different universe than the individual who believes "life is lack."

We are not espousing Donald Trump's lifestyle; nor do we believe the purpose of life is to gain money or possessions. We are merely pointing out that your internal, subconscious assumptions are going to form the very essence of how you walk through life.

Remember, the point of The Afformation Method is not to find "the answer" to your questions. Since you are now going to be forming positive questions that assume that what you want is already true, your mind will work to find a way to make it so.

Can you see how this process must, by definition, change your life?

HOW YOU'LL KNOW WHEN IT'S WORKING

The question we get most often about afformations is: "How will I know when it's working?" (This question, by the way, typically comes from people who haven't tried it consciously yet.) Many people who start using afformations report an almost instant feeling of calm and peace of mind that comes over them.

However, the Afformations Method is based on science, not magic. You cannot ask yourself, *"Why am I so thin and healthy?"* while continuing to eat unhealthy foods, and expect to lose weight. You cannot break the Laws of the Universe by sowing positive questions and continuing to do negative or self-defeating behaviors.

✳

You cannot break the Laws of the Universe by sowing positive questions, and continuing to do negative or self-defeating behaviors.

The point about using afformations is not to try and trick your mind, but to use it properly.

As we've noted, you're already using this method anyway, but most people are using it unconsciously, in a negative or self-defeating way.

Use afformations, but don't worry about doing them "right." There's more going on in the subconscious mind than science will ever be aware of. But using conscious afformations will enable your mind's Automatic Search Function to produce remarkable results in your favor, rather than negative ones you don't want.

HOW TO USE THE REST OF THIS BOOK

The rest of this book includes powerful afformations for the 10 major areas of building your practice, from Growing Your Practice with Integrity to Financial Abundance to Influencing Your Community and Giving Back. Of course, no single book could cover every afformation, because the number of afformations is literally infinite.

That's why we've left room between the afformations for you to write your own, personalized afformations that suit your individual situation. You can also refer to the other books in The Afformation Series (see Helpful Resources at the back of the book, or visit **SuccessClinic.com**)

Use them, go over them in your mind, read them again and again, and write them out as you would traditional "affirmations"– but notice that afformations may flow very easily for you!

That's because rather than trying to force yourself to believe something that you may not really believe, you'll be forming new assumptions about life and your relationship to it, based on what you really do want.

We know of no other method that can yield such dramatic results with so little effort.

And now, enjoy discovering your new incredibly simple questions – and reaping your amazingly powerful results!

4

AFFORMATIONS ON STARTING OUT

Youth is curious, and success is a game for
curiosity seekers. Stay young!
— B.J. Palmer

This is the most exciting time of your life! Hey, stop laughing — it's true. Whether you're in your early 20's just finishing school, or have gone back later in life to go for your dream, the beginning is beautiful! So sit back, take a deep breath, and look at what's really going on.

Sure, you have a lot of pressures to deal with: graduation, National Boards, student loans, where to set up practice, and so on. But you also have your

Dream – brand new, untarnished, and all yours.

That's why there's one thought we'd like you to keep with you with as you begin your journey:

You have within you Innate Intelligence and all around you, Infinite Intelligence.

You have God as your CEO, and the best part is…He's just waiting to be asked.

Give your practice to God and enjoy the ride. Always remember that you have everything you need to succeed. You are skilled, intelligent, gifted and motivated. Use the afformations in this chapter to give yourself permission to be wildly successful!

Why am I so creative and motivated?

Why do I resonate with the vision of chiropractic?

Why is my motivation accelerated each and every morning?

Why did I finish my senior year without fear?

Why am I so confident facing my
National Boards?

Why did I breeze through my National
Board exams on the first try?

Why do I so easily find a creative solution
to repay my student loans?

Why do I begin my practice with such
enthusiasm?

Why did I find the perfect place to practice?

Why is my office in the perfect location?

Why is my office well within my budget?

Why am I so confident in my work?

Why are my goals so firmly imbedded in my mind?

Why are my goals so achievable?

Why am I so excited about my goals?

Why are my goals becoming reality?

Why do I visualize my plan so vividly?

Why am I at peace with success?

Why is success so much fun?

Why am I so blessed to be a chiropractor?

Why is my commitment to success unstoppable?

Why did I refuse to hold myself back?

Why do I so easily attract new patients?

Why is every new patient so excited to
refer a friend?

Why is my practice growing beyond my
wildest dreams?

Why am I the best, most successful
chiropractor on the planet?

Why am I a perfect example of what a
chiropractor should be?

Why do I love what I do and do what I love?

Afformations on Starting Out

Why am I amazed at how quickly I'm
growing my practice?

Why is healing so rewarding?

Why am I so deserving of the practice of
my dreams?

Why are so many people supportive of my
vision, and want to help it come to pass?

Why am I a new patient magnet, attracting
new patients at will?

Why do patients and their families
come to me for lifetime care?

~ Don't be a passenger –
Get busy helping this craft along! ~

5

AFFORMATIONS ON FINDING YOUR BECAUSE

There is a power within, a fountainhead of unlimited resource, and he who controls it controls circumstances instead of it controlling him.
— B.J. Palmer

Finding Your Because is the term we use in our *Permission to Succeed®* workshops that means "find your mission" or understand why you're doing what you're doing.

Human behavior is determined by your Why-to's and Why-Not-To's. What do we mean? You can know how to do something and never let yourself do it. For example, you know how to drive a car, and if you wanted to, you could drive on the wrong side of the road. Why don't you? Because you know you'll get creamed if you do.

Most people we meet know exactly *what* they want to do. They have all the skill and talent needed to succeed and they go after what they want. Then how can we explain the fact that some people achieve their dreams and some don't? Because some have gone inside and found out *why* they want to succeed, what their motivating power is, and followed it.

As a chiropractor, you have a deeper awareness of the power of Innate Intelligence and Infinite Intelligence. This is your driving force within. Harness it, identify it, engage it and make it work for you. Make your Because so strong you can feel it with every part of your being.

Once you've identified your Because, share it. Together with your spouse and your staff, formulate it and write it down. Incorporate beliefs that are important to those who will share your dream. If they are a part of it, they will support it completely.

When you have a strong Because, you can then easily filter any decision through it and come up with an easy answer to most questions that will come your way using one simple question: *"Will this action I'm considering take me closer to or further away from my goal?"*

Asking this simple question can make tough decisions easier. If you're considering hiring someone, purchasing different equipment, changing your billing practices – whatever you may be worried about – just ask yourself that simple question and you will arrive at a simple answer.

Find Your Because and you'll find life opening its doors to you, through the power of intention and the gift of love.

Why do I live the Chiropractic dream?

Why does my dream center around the power of Above-Down, Inside-Out?

Why am I so confident in my purpose?

Why is my practice an extension of my being?

Why do I so easily express my purpose to others?

Why do I convey my purpose in everything I do?

Why am I so clear about my vision for my practice?

Why does my mission statement so clearly reflect my beliefs and desires?

Why do I process every decision I make asking myself if this decision will move me closer to my mission?

Why do I not get pulled away or detracted from my mission statement?

Why do I update my mission statement to reflect my current needs or beliefs?

Why do I include my mission statement in my morning and evening meditation?

Why do I always act in accordance with my mission statement?

Why do I view clear goals as my roadmap to success?

Why is God and His plan for me limitless?

Why is my plan attainable with God as my partner?

Why am I so unstoppable in my plan?

Why have I given myself *permission to succeed*?

Why does following my plan make me so happy?

Why does having a clear plan help my family to support me?

Why do I embrace success?

Why do I expect the best and allow the best to manifest in my life?

Why is my family so supportive of my goals?

Why am I empowered through Universal Intelligence?

Why do I place my trust in Universal Intelligence?

Why do I live the Chiropractic principle?

Why am I such a principled chiropractor?

Why do I get The Big Idea?

Why do lead others in getting The Big Idea,
so all else will follow?

Why am I on a mission?

Why AM I the mission?

*~There are two kinds of people in this world -
those who are always getting ready to do
something, and those who go ahead and do it.~*

6

AFFORMATIONS ON BUILDING YOUR PRACTICE WITH INTEGRITY

The difference between a good chiropractor and a poor one is that the good one has an ample supply of abstract principles in his head and the poor one only a few. Poor chiropractors are apt to substitute machinery for knowledge.

- Ralph Stephenson, D.C.

When you decided to become a chiropractor, why did you do it? Chances are, you did it because you were called to do it; because you have a strong desire to positively influence your fellow man; because you believe in higher values than the average person; because you believe in the power of Above-Down, Inside-Out; because you believe in Innate Intelligence and Infinite Intelligence. Right?

You are not just making a living; you are creating a legacy.

If you're not sure of your answer, you may want to re-examine your motives. Are your motives congruent with the fundamental philosophy of chiropractic? We've noticed that one of the subtle causes for unhappiness or lack of success is not being true to the integrity of your (any) profession.

It's easy to let go of your wonderful ideals when the bills pile up and you're facing setbacks or disappointments. What you have to keep in mind is the fact that you are not just making a living; you are creating a legacy.

Opportunities will arise that may look mighty tempting. For example, fuzzy billing practices, using modalities only to increase per visit fees, and billing for procedures that were not really necessary might net you a little more on the bottom line; but what are you really doing?

When you take from others without providing commensurate value, you are sending a message to the Universe that says, "I don't have, so I have to take." Guess what? The Universe responds with, "Fine, you don't have" and that will become your life.

Universal Intelligence is very literal; it reflects back to you what you put out. Therefore, if you put out the message of abundance and the belief that "I have enough", you will, in fact, receive abundance and have enough.

A belief in "not-enough" can often make a person lose sight of their integrity. It's much easier to start out on the right foot than to set a precedent that will be difficult to transition out of, both emotionally and physically, in the future.

Hold tight to your integrity and you will never go without. Stick to your vision and enjoy the abundance that is your heritage!

Why am I a doctor of integrity?

Why are all my decisions motivated by integrity?

Why do I not fall into the trap of suggesting unnecessary treatments just for the purpose of increasing fees?

Why are my billing practices fair and above board?

Why do I live a life that B.J. Palmer would be proud of?

Why do I always act in a way that would make my fellow Chiropractors proud?

Why do I protect the integrity of my Chiropractic profession?

Why do I act with dignity and honor?

Why does accountability make me so strong?

Why would I choose integrity over money in
making decisions?

Why do I always remember and appreciate the
higher purpose to which I've been called?

Why do I embrace the philosophy of healing the
body, mind and spirit from within?

Why does God walk with me in everything I do?

Why am I confident with God working as
my catalyst?

Why am I the vessel, and God the doer,
of my plan?

Why does God have all the answers along
my path?

Why will I serve God best by being my best?

Why do I treat my employees with such integrity?

Why does my joy as a leader come from empowering others?

Why do I enjoy growing as a leader?

Why does God direct me in becoming the best chiropractor ever?

Why do I love working in excellence?

Why is working in excellence who I really am?

Why do I listen carefully to all my patients?

Why do I keep my mind sharp and alert for the benefit of my family and patients?

Why do I love working with complete integrity?

Why do I care more about my patients than my income?

Why does my attention to detail promote peace of mind for both me and my patient?

Why am I so prompt and efficient in returning phone calls?

Why do I consider serving my patients an act of love?

Why do I serve my patients with the same courtesy I wish to receive?

Why am I so grateful for each and every one of my wonderful patients?

Why am I respected by my family?

Why do people want to emulate me?

Why am I safe to be Who I Really Am?

Why am I a perfect child of God?

Why am I a principled chiropractor, practicing specific chiropractic?

Why am I touching the masses with principled chiropractic?

Why do I remove the interference, so God can do the healing?

Afformations on Building Your Practice with Integrity

Why do I serve God best by being a success?

Why am I a mentor to my patients
and community?

Why is my community fortunate to have me
serving it?

Why do I walk my talk?

Why do I live the things I say?

*~ Seek first the kingdom of honesty,
and all the other graces acquire. ~*

7

AFFORMATIONS ON OVERCOMING FEAR, WORRY & FRUSTRATION

*Do not let fear collar you. There is no more
danger from lightning if you are running
than standing still.*
— B.J. Palmer

Y ou have heard many times that Fear is an acronym for False Evidence Appearing Real (or, as our friend Jack Canfield likes to say, "F--- Everything And Run!"). According to Dr. David Hawkins, Fear is a low level of consciousness, a paradigm of the universe that says,

"The world is a scary place." He writes in *Power vs. Force*: "The proliferation of fears is as limitless as the human imagination; once Fear is one's focus, the endless worrisome events of the world feed it."

Fear is an emotion created by disempowering questions you ask yourself; negative questions that begin with the phrase, "What if?":

"What if I can't make my loan payments...What if I never have enough patients...What if I'm not doing the right thing...What if...?"

Fear is not in itself a Cause; we cause it ourselves through our irrational, fear-based questions; the cycle feeds upon itself. When you view the world through the lens of Fear, the people, events and circumstances that could energize or excite, will cause worry and upset.

Mark Twain once said, "I am an old man and have known a great many troubles, but most of them

Fear is an emotion created by disempowering questions you ask yourself; negative questions that begin with the phrase, "What if?":

never happened."

Remember how 13-year-old Stefanie cured her chronic worrying by using afformations? If a little girl can do it, we know you can do it, too.

You really are stronger than you think you are. You are more capable than anyone, including yourself, may currently recognize. Begin asking yourself new questions about your ability to rise above fear, worry and frustration – and don't be surprised to see a brand new you springing forth!

Why do I face every day with confidence and courage?

Why does the power of Above-Down, Inside-Out give me such confidence and peace of mind?

Why are my partner and I successfully raising a healthy, happy, drug-free family?

Why does my partner desire to learn and
share Chiropractic principles and
philosophy together with me?

Why does my partner lovingly appreciate
that Chiropractic is not only a business,
but also a lifestyle?

Why do I view dead ends in my work as
powerful opportunities for new avenues
of creativity?

Why do I so easily turn setbacks into new
realms of success?

Why do I understand that what appear to
be roadblocks in my success, are just
opportunities for rediscovery or
regeneration?

Why does opposition from friends and family act to strengthen my core beliefs in what I do?

Why do I always seek new levels of wisdom?

Why am I fundamentally unstoppable in my quest for success?

Why do I so easily rise above those who are trying to hold me back?

Why do I face everyday with confidence, knowing I am enough?

Why do I completely enjoy the experience of everyday?

Why am I so safe to succeed?

Why does God want me to be blissfully
successful?

Why am I fearless because I live in a
house of faith?

Why did I finally quit worrying?

Why do I refuse to sabotage my own success?

Why does God erase my fears and make
my plans simple?

Why did I allow myself to get out of my
own way?

Why am I destined to succeed?

Why do I have so much worth and value?

Why do I trust myself to be the best
caregiver possible?

Why am I more confident with each new
patient I serve?

Why am I so respected in my career and life?

Why do I rise above unfair criticism?

Why am I so calm?

Why do I have more faith than fear?

Why am I good enough, even if I'm not
perfect?

Why am I a loved child of God?

Why do I have so much natural self-confidence?

Why do I feel so good sharing my
talents with the world?

Why do I trust Innate Intelligence enough to be
the best chiropractor possible?

Why do people value and appreciate me?

Why am I enough, just as I am?
(or as B.J. Palmer would say,
"Why am I enuf?")

*~ Action will remove the doubt
that theory cannot solve. ~*

8

AFFORMATIONS ON ORGANIZING & DELEGATING

Throw away your wishbone,
straighten up your backbone,
stick out your jawbone and go to it.
- B.J. Palmer

Mary Melissa, a sales professional, came to our *Permission to Succeed*® workshop because she wanted to get rid of the blocks she felt were holding her back from success. After working with us for a short time on building her Systems of Support™, she realized that her biggest physical block was the clutter in her office.

We advised her to start small and get rid of one

thing a day for the next seven days. She took our advice, then went one better – she took out seven *garbage bags* of stuff she no longer wanted!

With the clutter gone, she was able to stop wasting time trying to locate files and order forms, and was able to focus on important activities like selling, marketing and customer service.

Within a few short weeks, her commission checks had increased so much that she was able to re-paint several rooms in her house and replace the carpet in her office – the one she couldn't even see before!

There are three commodities in the human realm. Every action we take, everything we do, and everything we will ever do involves one or more of these commodities. The three human commodities are: Time, Energy, and Money.

Of these, which is the most valuable?

The answer, of course, is Time. Why? Because it's the only one that can never be replaced. (All of Bill Gates's billions can't buy one minute of yesterday.)

The secret to maximizing your most valuable commodity is one simple word: leverage. When you delegate, you're gaining leverage on your storehouse of Time, and when you organize, you're saving Time you would otherwise have wasted in unproductive activities.

Remember, Time itself is infinite, but our experience of Time is finite. You have 86,400 seconds each day to do with as you choose; use the questions below to get the most out of every one of them. (Quick– there goes another one!)

Why do I empower my staff to do their jobs?

Why do I spend more time planning my
life than my vacation?

Why am I so perfectly organized?

Why are all my systems working perfectly?

Why do I delegate with confidence?

Afformations on Organizing & Delegating

Why do I love being organized?

Why does organization make success easier?

Why do I hire people with gifts and
talents to keep me organized?

Why do I have a place for everything and
keep everything in its place?

Why does my office run more smoothly because
of how efficiently I delegate duties?

Why do I easily delegate tasks that can be
done well by others?

Why do I cherish the freedom that comes
from not trying to do and be everything
to everyone?

Why do I allow myself time to focus on growing my practice and caring for my patients?

Why are my patients better served now that I've relinquished clerical duties?

Why am I maximizing my time to build my practice rather than trying to do everything?

Why is it OK to let go?

Why is delegating the only way to build a strong practice?

Why does my staff represent me so well?

Why does everyone want to imitate my life of order and organization?

Why am I free from chaos and clutter?

Why do I complete all of my tasks on time?

Why does my new freedom give me
energy and drive?

Why do I view systems and order as part
of a strong practice?

Why is a life of order a life of peace?

Why do I enjoy better health and peace of
mind through organization?

Why do I take full advantage of proven
systems to streamline my business?

Why has my practice grown beyond belief
now that I have freed myself of
unnecessary burdens?

Why do I give myself permission to delegate and organize?

Why have I built a larger, stronger practice through my example of organization and delegation?

Why are the best employees attracted to me?

Why do I treat my staff with such respect and fairness?

Why do I treat my staff as extensions of me?

Why do I train my staff and give them the tools to succeed?

Why do I realize a well-trained staff creates a successful practice?

Why do I always lead by example?

Why do I build and encourage team spirit
and unity within my staff?

Why do I lead and help others reach their goals?

Why do I encourage my staff to grow and learn?

Why do I lead with a giving spirit?

Why am I so well-prepared to serve the masses?

Why am I masterful at maximizing my time?

Why do I not just prioritize my schedule, but
schedule my priorities?

Why am I so profoundly proactive?

Why am I so focused?

Why do I value my time?

Why do others value my time?

Why do I follow simple, efficient, and effective procedures and systems of success?

Why am I so comfortable in an atmosphere of volume and activity?

Why do I have such a capable, trustworthy team?

*~ To establish and maintain order,
harmony and excellence in the territory
under one's own hat,
will keep one fairly well occupied. ~*

9

AFFORMATIONS ON ATTRACTING CENTERS OF INFLUENCE

Keep your head cool – feet warm – mind busy.
Plan work ahead and stick to it – rain or
shine. If you are a gem, someone will find you.
– B.J. Palmer

D id you ever notice that sometimes you can walk up to someone and immediately feel connected or attracted to them, and other times feel repelled? What you're feeling is very real and very tangible. You are actually experiencing your body's natural reaction to that person's aura – the measurable energy field surrounding a person.

✳

*Are you
trying to
create a true
win/win
situation,
or are you
looking only
at what you
can gain?*

Have you stopped to think how your own aura could be attracting or repelling influential people? Have you taken the time to find out where your heart and your intention are before approaching those who could substantially influence your future and your career?

Are you having self-serving thoughts, or are you trying to create a situation where you would not only receive from this person, but could also give back in some way? Are you trying to create a true win/win situation, or are you looking only at what you can gain?

When you approach each person you meet with a selfless heart and a good intention, they will pick up on that intention and experience a magnetic attraction to you and your cause.

Before you know it, you'll realize that you have

always been surrounded by oceans of helpful souls ready and willing to enrich your life. You'll be amazed to see how Infinite Intelligence has positioned the help you need at your fingertips and how easily you will recognize it.

Choose your mentors wisely. Surround yourself with people you really want to emulate. Be certain that their philosophy aligns with yours. Remember, nothing is worth compromising your integrity.

Keep in mind what we said in the chapter on *Finding Your Because* about making sure that actions you take will move you towards your goal, not away. This is especially important in choosing those you decide to align yourself with. Remember that you will be judged by those with whom you associate.

We've created these afformations to enable you to trust your instincts and go forward with confidence. Enjoy!

Why do others feel my incredible passion
for my profession?

Why do I confidently seek the advice of great chiropractors who have gone before me?

Why do I find wisdom in the words of my mentors?

Why do I magnetically attract people of influence?

Why does my expression of joy, health and purposeful living attract people who can help me reach my highest levels of success?

Why do I turn to doctors with experience to help me in areas where I may feel lack?

Why do people of influence desire to be in my space?

Why is it so easy to find the money I need?

Why am I always in the right place, doing the right thing with the right people at the right time?

Why does opportunity come to me so easily and so often?

Why are leaders so magnetically attracted to me?

Why am I so good at spotting opportunities and making the most of them?

Why are so many influential people eager to share my dream?

Why do people with high levels of influence show me great favor?

Why am I so supported by those who believe in me?

Why do I look forward to meeting new,
influential people?

Why do I allow myself to be put in the
path of great people who can help me?

Why do I remember to offer something first to
people from whom I desire assistance?

Why do I appreciate and not take
advantage of people who help me?

Why was the perfect mentor put in my path today?

Why do I learn from my mentors, so I can also
mentor others?

Why do I always view a stranger as just a
friend I haven't met yet?

Why do I seek to learn something valuable from every person I meet?

Why do I listen for the lesson in every meeting?

Why do I feel so confident striking up conversations with strangers?

Why are people of influence so happy to talk to me?

Why do I do my homework and make a great impression on influential people?

Why do I do my preparation to insure I make a great impression on people of influence?

Why do I always seek to create a win/win situation when seeking guidance?

Why do I seek to help others first?

Why does my sense of humor help me in
speaking with people of influence?

Why does God calm me when I approach someone
who seems to be "more powerful" than me?

Why do people follow me as a role model
for optimal health?

Why am I such a brilliant example of
God's abundance?

*~ When you begin to thirst for knowledge,
you drink it in. You need not go out for it.
The ocean of it surrounds us as the
atmosphere. ~*

10

AFFORMATIONS ON FINANCIAL ABUNDANCE & PROSPERITY

"Everything comes to him that waits;"
But here is one that's slicker:
The man who goes after what he wants
Gets it a darn sight quicker.
— B.J. Palmer

Here it is: the subject nobody wants to talk about — money. So, how much is enough? At what level are you rich? How much is it OK to have before you somehow offend the Universe?

The answers aren't what you would expect. It isn't about how much you have — for instance, one of our clients who took our success coaching was earning more than $600,000 per year, while another student in the same class was a beginning salesperson trying to move up from her $12,000 annual income.

Your *attitude* about money is determined by your *relationship* to money. You may be telling yourself outwardly that you have a great attitude – you want it and you want lots of it and you want it now – but what if, on the inside, you're hearing other voices?

What if, for example, you grew up in a family where money was associated with evil or negative things? One of our clients, a middle aged man, began to cry during one of our seminars when we discussed the subject of money and finances. When we asked him about it, he had a most powerful story to tell:

Your attitude about money is determined by your relationship to money.

He said his dad had grown up during the Depression and had ingrained in him that all white-collar workers were to blame for the burdens put on the blue-collar workers, and they were the enemy. His father was a blue-collar worker and their family lived on small means in a tiny apartment.

Our client had gotten married and also lived in a small apartment, but a voice inside him told him there was a better way. He worked hard to provide a better life for his family, moving up the ladder of success. After several years, he was finally able to purchase a modest home for his wife and kids. He kept his plans a secret from his mom and one day, proudly picked her up and drove her over to see the new home.

He knew she would be so proud of him for what he had done and he was so excited to escort her through. She walked in silence, but tears streamed down her face as she passed from room to room. He smiled and said, "What is it, Mom? What do you think?" She turned to him and said, "Son, I'm just glad that your father didn't live to see this day. You ought to be ashamed."

It can be very difficult to escape the attitudes you were raised with concerning money, unless you can first identify the voices you're hearing and then come to terms with them and form your own relationship to it.

Infinite Intelligence has set up the Universe so that there is no lack.

Suppose you always heard things like, "Money doesn't grow on trees" or "Don't ask for things, you know we're broke" or "Make sure to save your money because you never know when your life will fall apart and you'll need it." Some of these may sound ridiculous at first, but think about it: were you raised with an attitude of abundance, or one of lack?

If you were raised with a lack mentality, then you must take a good hard look at what you've experienced and realize it doesn't have to be that way. Infinite Intelligence has set up the Universe so that there is no lack. The Universal Plan is that there is plenty for everyone. Wealth is not a negative thing that only bad or selfish people have. Bill and Melinda Gates are two of the richest people in the world; they have blessed millions of people through their foundation. They have much and they give in good proportion.

If you were fortunate enough to be raised with an abundant mentality (note, we didn't say an abundant <u>checkbook</u>), you know for certain that you will always be taken care of and you truly will never want. Placing your faith and your life in the hands of Infinite Intelligence is the best guarantee of living a life of true abundance, one that can't always be measured in dollars and cents.

If life brings you abundant wealth, enjoy it and remember to give back. Never measure your worth by the number on your bank statement.

We invite you to use the following afformations to form a healthy attitude of abundance and a good relationship with money. May you be blessed with a most abundant life!

Why is my practice so financially sound?

Why does accountability make me strong?

Why does what I have never take away from, but only enrich, the lives of others?

Why is money so happy to be with me?

Why is having an abundance of patients so easy for me?

Why am I so relaxed because my schedule book is always filled exactly how I want it?

Why do I enjoy finding new and creative ways to bring in new patients?

Why does the healthy income I make from my full schedule take so much pressure off of my family?

Why do banks and financial institutions
see my value and work with me to find
creative solutions to my financial needs?

Why is my family so proud of the success
that I am?

Why am I so well rewarded for my work?

Why do I invest my time and money
wisely, seeking sound advice?

Why do I attract money, prosperity and
abundance to me?

Why do I tithe 10% with love?

Why do I always have more to share and
give away?

Why do I excel and accomplish with such effortless ease?

Why do I give myself permission to prosper?

Why does money come to me so easily?

Why do I accept abundance with an attitude of gratitude and sharing?

Why do I grow my wealth in perfect proportion, both financial and spiritual?

Why am I a happy, sharing, caring money magnet?

Why do I sow and reap in wild abundance?

Why do I reap such a bountiful harvest with the many rich seeds I have sown?

Why am I so easily debt-free?

Why is it OK to be both wealthy and spiritual?

Why is my value not a reflection of my
bank statement?

Why do I not define my life by the
amount of money I earn?

Why do I happily accept wealth as a vessel
to reach and help others?

Why do my spouse/partner and I communicate
so well about financial values?

Why do I always have more than enough?

Why am I always at peace knowing my
practice is led by Infinite Intelligence?

NOAH ST. JOHN & DENISE BÉRARD

Why do I teach my children the fine art of giving?

Why do I never use the words *"poor, not enough, broke, we don't have, or lack"* in front of my children?

Why do I teach my children that, through Infinite Intelligence, there is always enough?

Why do I trust that God will provide?

Why do I dedicate my practice to Infinite Intelligence knowing that abundance will surely follow?

Why is God my CEO?
Why does the abundance in my life allow me to do more charitable work?

Why has God given me the power to
attain great wealth?

Why am I such a savvy investor?

Why do I not worry, working through the
power of Infinite Intelligence?

Why am I so abundantly taken care of?

Why am I more than enough, therefore I
attract more than enough?

*~ In loaning money, the moral character
of the borrower counts for more
than his financial worth.
Get busy on your character. ~*

11

AFFORMATIONS ON
PATIENT APPRECIATION

*I know that a certain attitude of mind
and habit of action on my part will add
to the peace, happiness and well being of other people.*
- B.J. Palmer

What is a practice if not a bouquet of patients? Each and every patient is its own special flower in this bouquet. Each comes with his own special style, color, fragrance, personality and intention. Treat each one as if they were your only one.

Your patients are truly your sales force. They are your volunteer team just waiting to champion your cause. Every patient wants to have the best story of how you restored them to health or helped them turn their lives around.

They come to you with hope, anticipation, respect and sometimes even fear. Nurture them, give them the best care you can, and educate them so they may have a better life, not just temporary relief from pain.

Many times it's not how you outwardly treat your patients, it's about your inner feelings. Are you always happy to see them? Are you sincerely concerned about their issues? Do you know them each as individuals? Do you make an effort to say something to make them feel better about themselves, not just about their health or condition? Do you consciously listen to what they're saying?

Your intentions are broadcast to and known by others, even when you don't say them. Dr. David Hawkins, author of *Power vs. Force*, did experiments with groups of up to 1,000 people. In a double-blind study, he gave half the group sealed envelopes filled with pure organic vitamin C, and the other half envelopes filled with artificial sweetener.

Test subjects were told to hold the envelopes against their solar plexus while they were given a strength test. In 100% of cases, the group holding artificial sweetener all tested weaker than those holding the natural Vitamin C. The *being* knows, even when the conscious mind is unaware.

Everything is connected in some way to Innate Intelligence through Infinite Intelligence. Everything you think, do, feel and say will ultimately impact the mental and physical health and well-being of your patients.

Think good thoughts: thoughts of appreciation, compassion and hope. Show your patients often how they are appreciated. When patients leave your office feeling positive, they will be compelled to share their find (you) with friends.

The strongest practices are grown in the fertile soil of patient appreciation. Tend to each patient and your harvest will be plentiful!

Why do I see each patient as a precious partner?

Why am I so committed to making each patient feel important?

Why do I hold my patients lovingly accountable for their role in their care?

Why do I make a point of remembering each patient's name?

Why do I inquire about at least one thing about each patient that is personally important to them?

Why do I take the time to instruct my patients in the best practices that will create a healthy life?

Why do I give every patient the tools they need for a healthy, balanced lifestyle?

Why do my patients feel better about themselves just being around me?

Why do I protect the integrity and privacy
of my patients?

Why is my mission not only to restore
health, but also to educate?

Why does my honest and sincere desire to
provide the best care come through loud
and clear to each patient?

Why am I efficient, yet caring with every patient?

Why am I the best listener I know?

Why do patients easily see the benefit I
bring to them and their families?

Why do I enjoy working closely with my
patients to make sure my treatment is
efficient and effective?

Why do I always remember an empowered patient is a return patient who refers others?

Why do I try to connect with light-heartedness, humor and warmth to all my patients?

Why do my patients immediately sense how much I love my work?

Why do I easily ask for referrals?

Why do my patients view me as a mentor and partner in their plan for health?

Why do I have such a calming effect on my patients and staff?

Why do I instill such confidence in my patients?

Why do I always remember that a confident doctor creates a trusting patient?

Why do I easily replace all fear with knowledge and understanding in the minds of my new patients?

Why do my patients appreciate the time and attention I give them?

Why does every new patient I meet help me to grow my practice so easily?

Why do I appreciate every patient, knowing that they are truly my sales force?

Why do I respect my patients's choices?

Why do I appreciate that *word of mouth* is my best advertising?

Why do I take the time to instruct each new patient in the basic principles and philosophy of Chiropractic, so they can be knowledgeable when they speak to others to spread the word?

Why is every patient so excited to give me referrals?

Why does each of my patients recommend me to at least one new family each week?

Why do patients appreciate my sincerity, enthusiasm and caring?

Why are my patients so comfortable passing my name on to friends?

Why do I find creative ways to reward patients for referrals?

Why do I genuinely show my appreciation
for referrals?

Why is every patient so excited and willing
to bring in their family to be checked for
subluxation?

Why do I realize and appreciate that the
opportunity I provide may be the answer
to someone's prayers?

Why do I see every referral as the opportunity to
change someone's life for the better?

Why am I so grateful to be changing so
many people's lives for the better?

Why do I celebrate my patients?

Why can I say more by saying less?

Afformations on Patient Appreciation

Why am I a master at doing Patient
Appreciation Days?

Why am I a master at showing love and
appreciation?

Why am I so proud to serve through the
vehicle of principled, specific, scientific
Chiropractic?

Why do I inspire others to be their best by
being my best?

Why am I so passionate about chiropractic and
sharing it with everyone I meet?

Why do I unconditionally love my patients
and my family?

Why do I always say the right things?

Why do I tell the truth to my patients
about their condition?

Why do I give every patient my utmost
Present Time Consciousness (PTC)?

*~ The prophet without honor is the one
who does not know how to advertise. ~*

12

AFFORMATIONS ON BALANCING FAITH, FAMILY & CAREER

Health is an achievement.
If you want it, you have to say so,
then work for it.
– B.J. Palmer

We believe God's plan for you is very simple: to Be and Express Who You Really Are, and to serve others through that Expression.

As a chiropractor, you certainly know the benefit of balance – within your body, in your diet, between your mind, body and spirit. But have you actually made the time to plan for balance between your Faith, your

Family and your Career? This is often one of the greatest challenges; to realize what God wants for our lives and then to just do it!

What makes you feel rich? Happy? Fulfilled? As much as you've heard about this before, it really is not dependent on having an amount of money. We've met people earning in the high six figures who feel miserable, and those making a lot less who are blissfully happy.

True happiness, peace of mind and contentment comes from only one thing – Balance.

Having that rich, happy, fulfilled feeling comes from doing what you're here to do. Use these afformations to help you live the life you were meant to live.

Why do I appreciate that chiropractic isn't just a job, it's a way of life?

Why does my family joyfully share my Chiropractic philosophy?

Afformations on Balancing Faith, Family & Career

Why do I carefully balance my love of
chiropractic with my love of family?

Why do I lovingly include my family in my career?

Why do I involve my children in the
Chiropractic Way?

Why do I remember to keep a special place
in my heart just for my family?

Why can I be happy and complete even if
all my friends or family don't share my
love of Chiropractic?

Why does my love for my family continue
to grow as I build my practice?

Why does my spouse/partner understand
where my passion comes from?

Why am I creating not only a practice, but also building a legacy?

Why do I find beauty in everyday life?

Why am I so creative in making my relationships special?

Why is my family so excited about helping me achieve my goals?

Why do I keep special time and do special things for my spouse/partner to show them how much I care?

Why do I put my faith and my family first, knowing I will have a life of success?

Why do I work better and laugh more when I take time for me?

Why do I carefully plan my day and my
life to include a good balance of faith,
family and career?

Why do I treat my practice with the
respect and enthusiasm it deserves?

Why do I treat my family with the respect
and enthusiasm they deserve?

Why do I so easily plan my work and
work my plan?

Why are my results astounding when I work by
commitment and manage my time?

Why is my life in balance and order?

Why do I have the perfect balance of life
outside of my practice?

Why did I stop going for perfection and instead, go for peace of mind, balance and harmony?

Why does my life reflect perfect balance and harmony now?

Why is God so happy for me?

Why do I do just enough work and just enough play?

Why is the order of my life faith first, family second and career third?

Why did I stop feeling guilty for taking time off from work?

Why am I the best spouse, parent and chiropractor?

Why do I have such a happy, healthy family life?

Why is my family so supportive of me and
my efforts?

Why am I an understanding spouse and parent?

Why do I love my family, warts and all?

Why do I catch my spouse/partner and
children doing something right everyday?

Why am I so supportive of my children?

Why are my children so supportive of me?

Why am I so supportive of my spouse/
partner?

Why is my spouse/partner so wonderful?

Why do I live in such a peaceful home?

Why do I check and adjust my family regularly?

Why do I give my family the best
chiropractic care?

Why do I spend time reading the Green
Books daily?

Why do I spend time with God daily?

Why do I enjoy one day of rest each week?

Why do I enjoy a date with my spouse/partner
every week?

Why is my life so perfect and perfectly
wonder-filled?

Why do I appreciate the wonderful family
I've been blessed with?

Why am I so happy, healthy, wealthy and wise?

Why is my life such a joyous adventure?

Why is my life filled with light, love,
marvelous people and fun times?

Why is life so fulfilling for me?

*~ The measure of a man's worth
is based on how successful he was able
to make others. ~*

13

AFFORMATIONS ON INFLUENCING YOUR COMMUNITY & GIVING BACK

Enter to learn how. Go forth to serve
– B.J. Palmer

At the heart of chiropractic philosophy is the importance of giving back. Chiropractors have always prided themselves on taking the holistic approach to healing, which combines the elements of the mind, body and spirit.

From its inception, the chiropractic philosophy was about helping, healing and promoting a better lifestyle through Infinite Intelligence. It stands to reason, therefore, that in order to fulfill the calling, a

NOAH ST. JOHN & DENISE BÉRARD

faithful chiropractor is always aware of his town, his community, and the world around him.

The most wonderful benefit of living a life of giving is the reality that the more we give and do for others, the more will come back to us.

Denise says: My Dad was the perfect example of a chiropractor who lived this philosophy. He was not only a wonderful doctor; he was a humble, giving, spiritually centered husband and father.

He ran his business using the "GPC" philosophy: God, Patient, Chiropractor. He had a box on the wall and his patients would put whatever they could afford in the box as payment. Many weeks we received free car washes, afghans, vegetables from someone's farm stand, whatever his patients could afford to give. We were wealthy with an inner wealth that many may not be able to understand.

My Dad would spend his Saturdays making house calls to shut-ins and then he'd go to the rectory and convent and adjust the religious, all at no charge. He received a Papal Commendation for his dedication to the community and his generous, giving spirit.

It's so true that what you sow you will also reap. Later in his practice, he developed cataracts in both eyes, completely lost his vision, and required surgery. Three chiropractors from town came to his rescue and each took one full day out of their practices each week to come and care for my Dad's patients until he was fully recuperated. They each gave him the entire amount that they collected.

Later, my Dad developed cancer and could no longer work. Out of the blue, a childhood friend with whom he had started a print shop at the age of 16, came to the door and handed him a check for $16,000. That was a lot of money back then! Even though my Dad hadn't worked the shop in over 40 years, his friend had just sold the business and insisted on giving him half of what he received, stating, "We started this business together, we're going out together."

When my Dad passed away, the wake was extended to three days because the line of mourners continued non-stop from 2:00 p.m. to 10:00 p.m. each day.

My Dad left behind a legacy. He taught by example

and always walked the talk. After his passing, Life University honored him by engraving his name in their Bell Tower honoring the pioneers in chiropractic.

We've included the following series of afformations that will help you to turn great thoughts outward, so you can truly serve those around you. By just reading them through, can't you feel the power of these words?

Why does my joy as a leader come from empowering others?

Why do I lead by coaching others to reach their goals?

Why do I enjoy helping others become leaders?

Why is it such a privilege to be a leader in this community?

Why do I always give back in gratitude for
what I've been blessed with?

Why is my practice the perfect venue for
me to express and enjoy my leadership
qualities?

Why does my leadership impact my
community, both social and spiritual, in
such a positive way?

Why do I get to express Who I Really Am
and receive such marvelous abundance as
a result?

Why does what I have never take away
from, but only enrich, the lives of others?

Why do I consistently exceed my expected
goals each and every week?

NOAH ST. JOHN & DENISE BÉRARD

Why do I give and receive in such joyful abundance?

Why am I always more rewarded when I give from the Heart?

Why is God so happy with me?

Why do I find such joy in mentoring others?

Why do I gratefully give back to the college that gave me my wonderful education?

Why am I a supportive alumnus?

Why do I find needs in my community and fill them?

Why do I set aside money each week to help support someone in need?

Why do I give of my time to causes that I support?

Why do I give back to my country in a way that means something to me?

Why do I give advice and support to chiropractic students so they may continue to bless the world?

Why am I so abundantly blessed for the blessings I happily bestow on others?

Why am I compassionate to those in need?

Why do I humbly give?

Why am I so willing and able to lessen the burdens of others?

Why do I find such peace and strength in supporting others?

Why do I find creative ways to give back without looking for personal praise?

Why do I always remember the first thing I learned in kindergarten - be nice and share?

Why am I so honored when asked for help or support?

~ The desire to partake and to contribute must balance each other. ~

14

FINAL THOUGHTS

A good question is never answered.
It is not a bolt to be tightened into place,
but a seed to be planted and to bear more seed
toward the hope of greening the landscape of idea.
– Henry David Thoreau

Our sincere hope is that you'll use the method and the afformations we've shared with you in this book to let yourself become wildly successful in your life, career and relationships. We've had the privilege of seeing thousands of people's lives turn around as a result of asking themselves new, empowering questions.

Many people have asked us how they can record empowering afformations to listen to as they go through their day.

That's why we developed **Just Ask Me™ Mind Makeover Software**. With just the click of a mouse, you can easily record your own afformations, set them to your favorite music, and play them in your car, on your computer, or virtually anywhere!

Just Ask Me also makes a great gift for friends, family and patients. (Ask the authors to tell you how they got on CNN using Just Ask Me!)

Get the inside scoop at **SuccessClinic.com.**

We'd love to hear your experiences working with afformations!

We're currently working on more books in the *Afformations*® and *Permission to Succeed*® series and would love to include your success story.

Send us your success story via email to: **stories@SuccessClinic.com.** *Ask away!*

HELPFUL RESOURCES

Alessandra, Tony. *The Platinum Rule.* Warner, 1998.

Hawkins, David. *Power vs. Force.* Hay House, 2002.

St. John, Noah & Berard, Denise. *Just Ask Me Mind Makeover Software.* Set afformations to your favorite music and manifest your desires directly from Infinite Intelligence. For the inside scoop, visit **www.SuccessClinic.com**

———. *The Great Little Book of Afformations*® MetaPublishing, 2006 (New Expanded Edition)

———. *Permission to Succeed*®. HCI, 2nd ed. 2004.

Vitale, Joe. *The Attractor Factor.* Wiley & Sons, 2005.

Wilkinson, Bruce. *The Dream Giver.* Multnomah, 2003.

Zimmerman, Scott. The Cyrano System: Marketing Intelli-Gently. **www.TheCyranoGroup.com**

WHO ARE NOAH ST. JOHN and DENISE BERARD?

Noah St. John and **Denise Bérard** are Founder and CEO of The Success Clinic of America, a Boston-based productivity company. Independent business professionals and multinational organizations in over 30 countries are using their methods to enjoy more control over their business, more freedom to do what they love, and more abundance in every aspect of life.

Noah is the author of two bestselling books including **Permission to Succeed®,** now in its 10th printing.

Denise is former Vice President of Sales for one of New England's most respected printing companies, where she doubled the company's revenues in less than 24 months. She brings over 20 years experience in sales management and consulting.

Who Are Noah St. John & Denise Bérard?

Jack Canfield of **CHICKEN SOUP FOR THE SOUL®** calls Noah & Denise's programs "one of the most significant breakthroughs in the study of success in decades."

Noah & Denise have been featured in *PARADE, Woman's Day, Los Angeles Business Journal, Washington Post, Chicago Sun-Times, Selling Power, Money Makers Monthly, Bottom Line/Personal, National Public Radio,* and ABC, CBS, NBC and Fox News.

For more information on their programs and products, visit them online at:

SuccessClinic.com

Write or call:

The Success Clinic of America
**1350 Lakeview Avenue, Dracut MA 01826
(978) 957-9999**

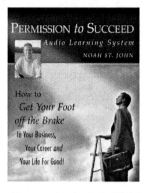

Permission to Succeed® Audio Learning System

Get all 7 steps to give yourself *permission to succeed!*

• 6 CDs or Cassettes
• Bonus Afformation CD
• CD: $129.95
• Tape: ~~$99.95~~ Now $49.95

Just Ask Me™ Mind Makeover Software

Set your afformations to your favorite music and listen in your car, on your computer, or anywhere!
• PC compatible
• $49.95

To order,
visit SuccessClinic.com
or call (978) 957-9999

More Resources to Help You Live The Life of Your Dreams!

Permission to Succeed®

The book that started it all!

• Remove self-sabotage for good
• Eliminate negative self-talk
• Gain more control over your life
• Enjoy more abundance
• $10.95 (HCI, New edition 2004)

The Great Little Book of Afformations® - New EXPANDED Edition!

Learn the secret of afformations and how to change your life using empowering questions.

• New Foreword by Dr. Joe Vitale, bestselling author, *The Attractor Factor*
• $12.95 (MetaPublishing, 2006)

To order,
visit SuccessClinic.com
or call (978) 957-9999

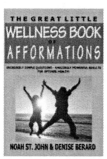
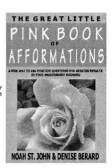

Coming Soon
from
Noah St. John & Denise Berard!

The Great Little Baby Book of Afformations®

The Great Little Millionaire's Book of Afformations®

Permission to Love™: How to Stop Sabotaging Your Relationships

...and more!

For all the latest updates,
products and seminars,
sign up for our
FREE newsletter
at **SuccessClinic.com**

Or call **(978) 957-9999**

Notes